SPOOKY SWEETS

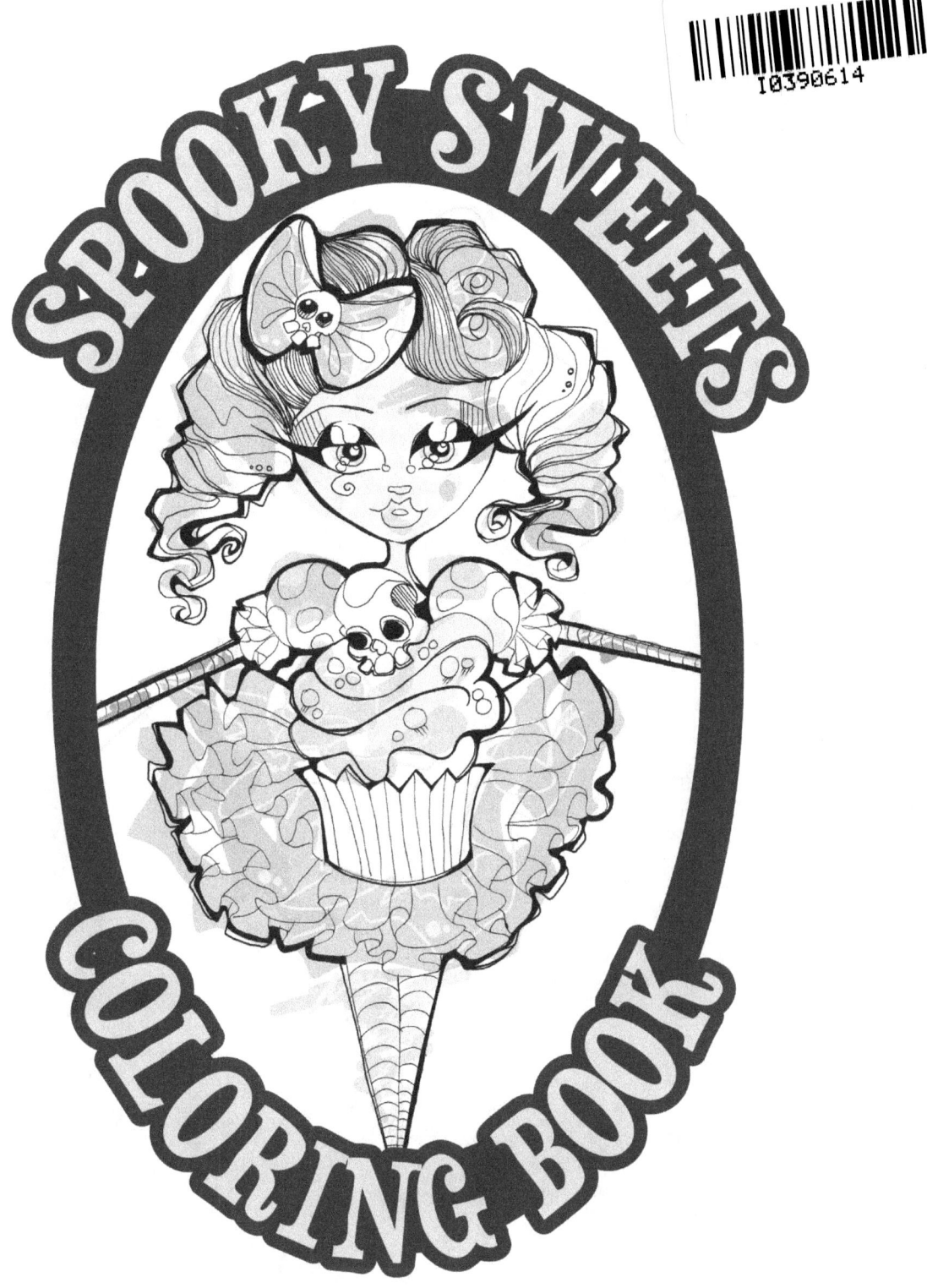

COLORING BOOK

Illustrated by Karla Magaña

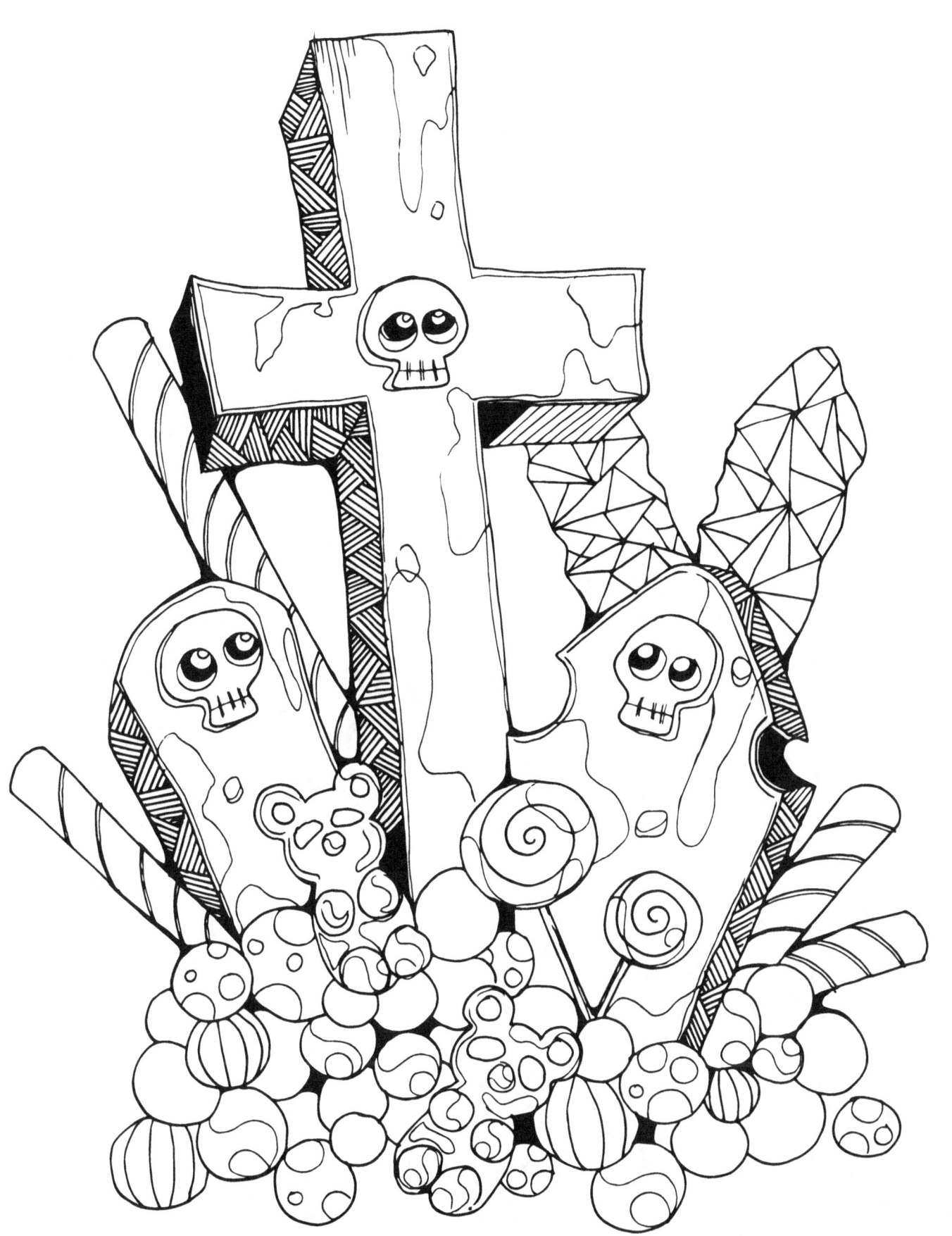

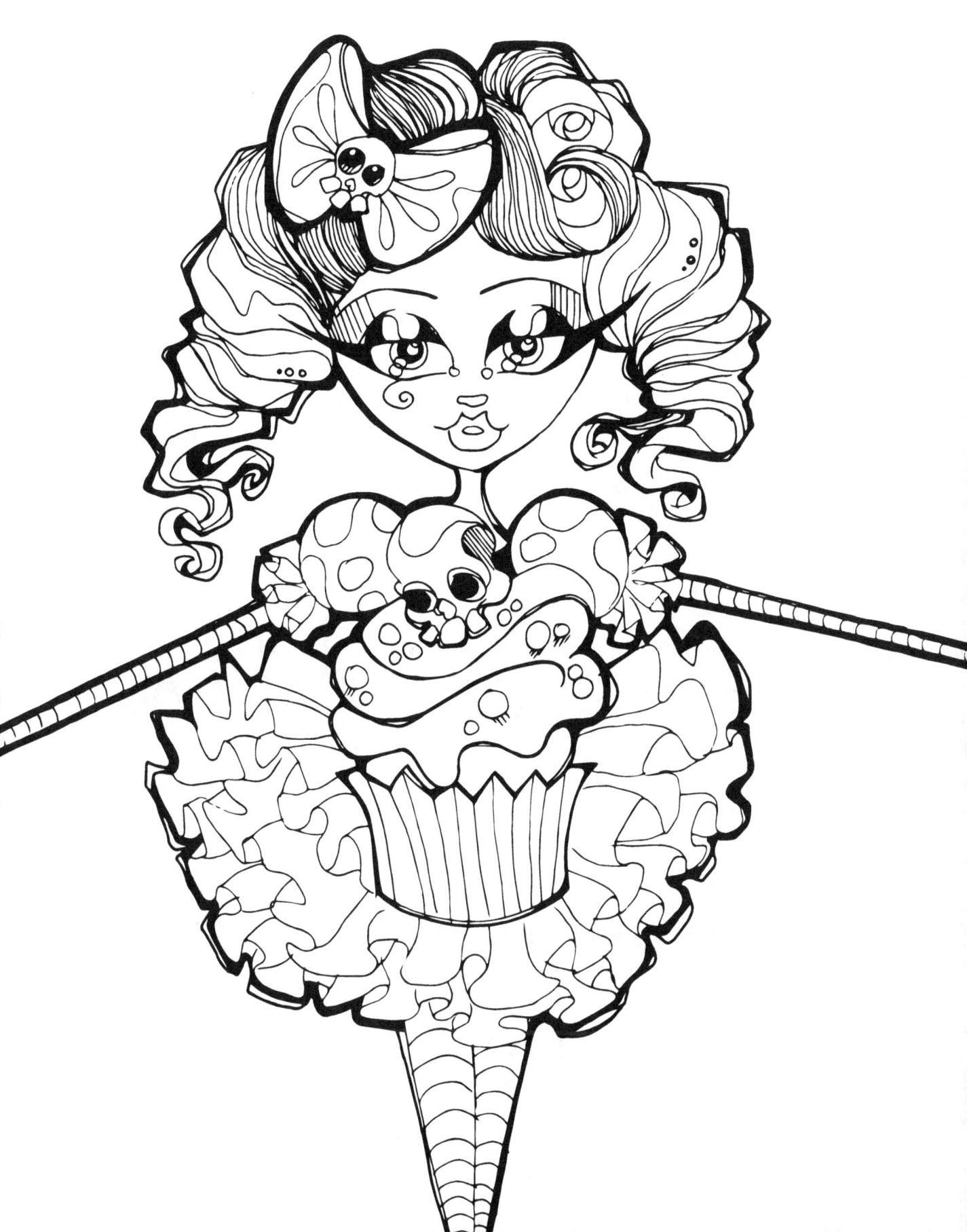

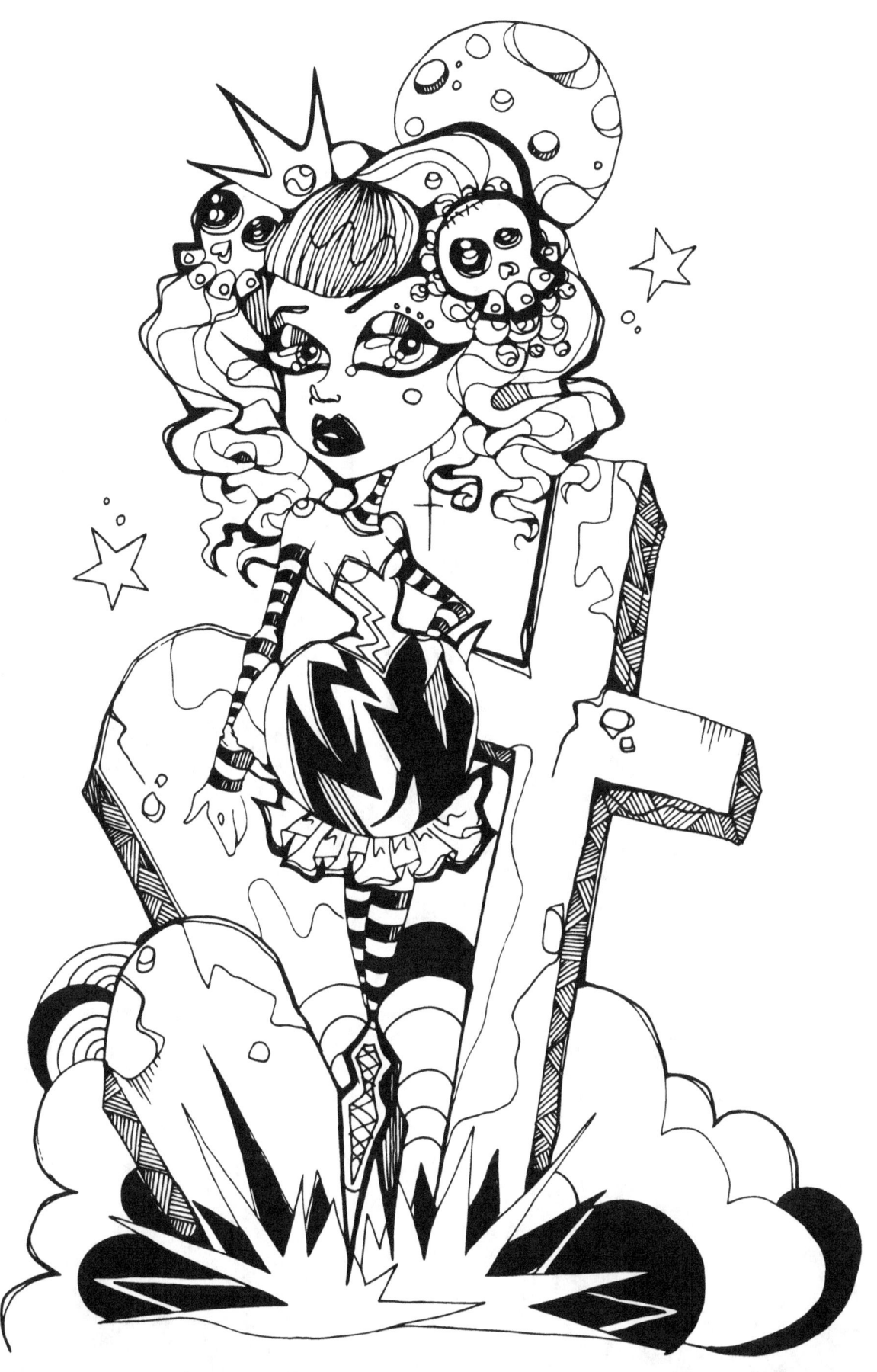

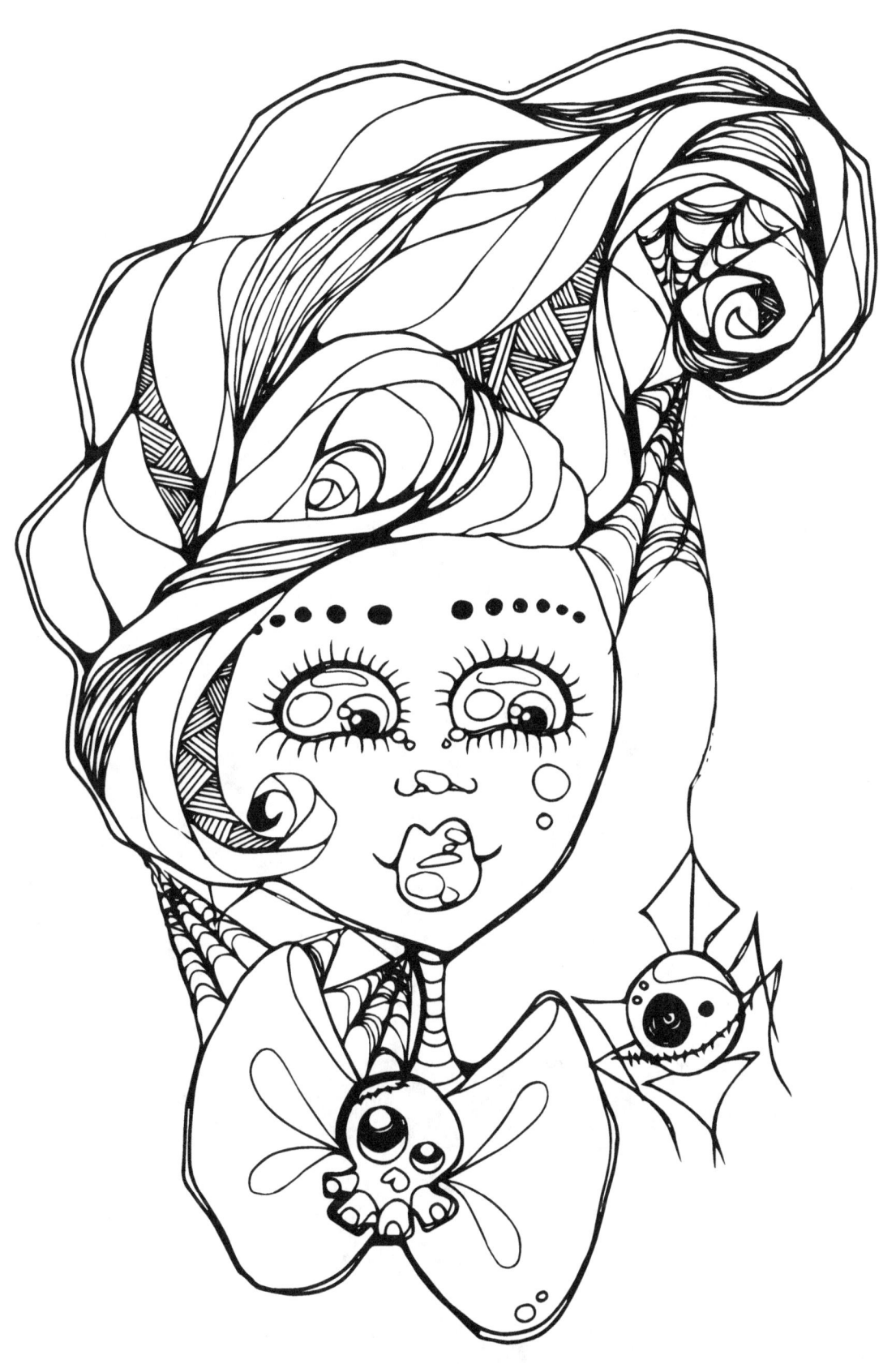

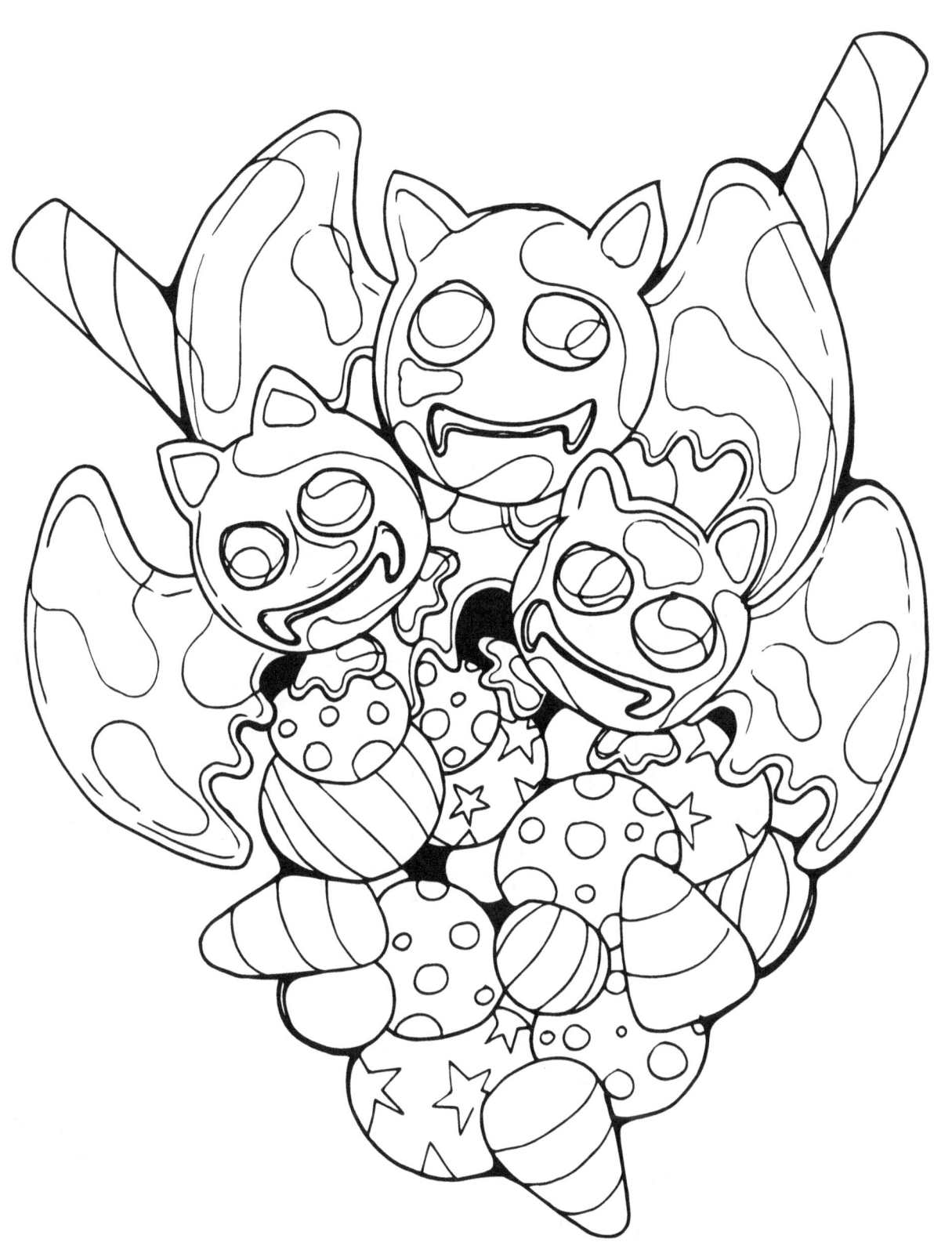

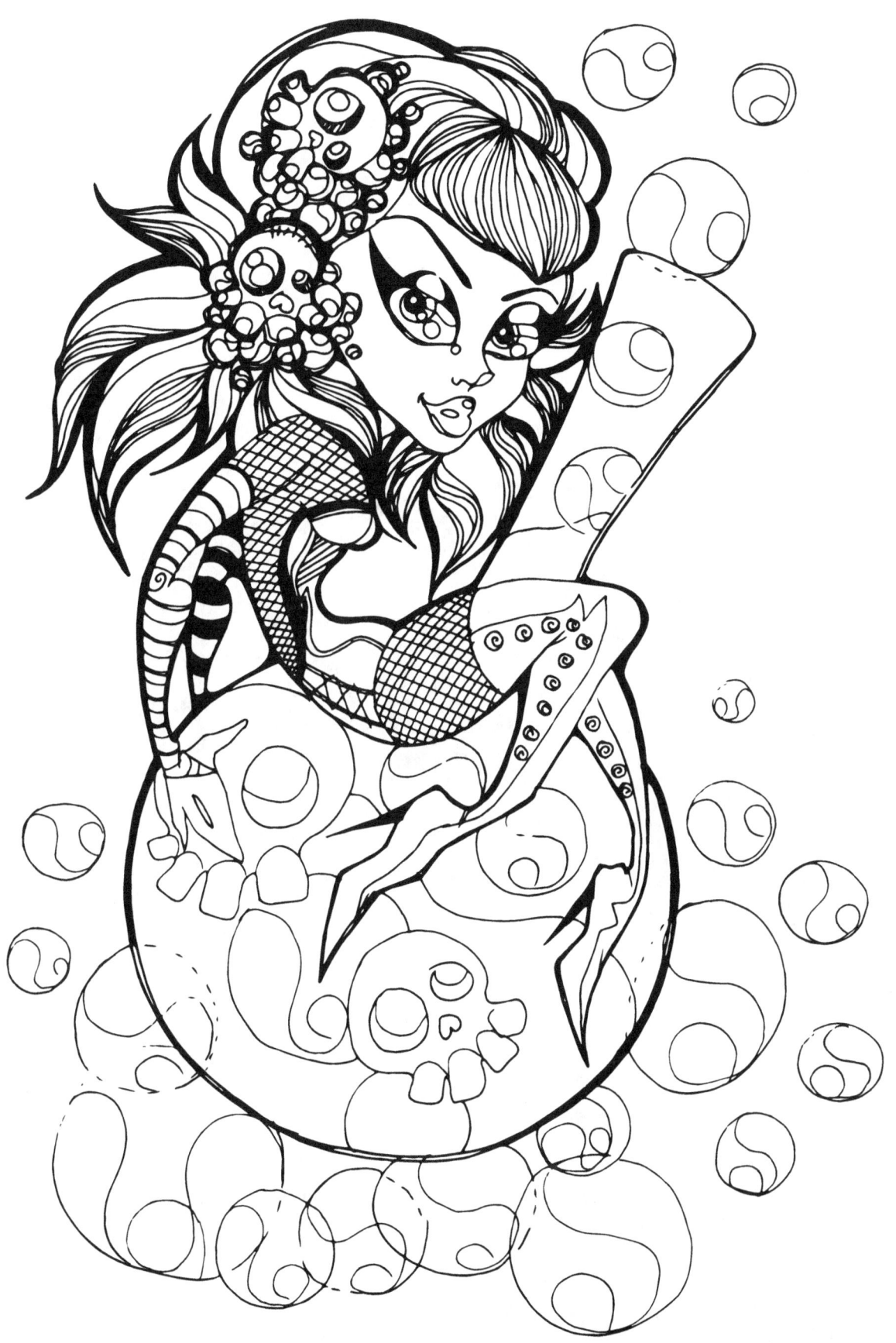

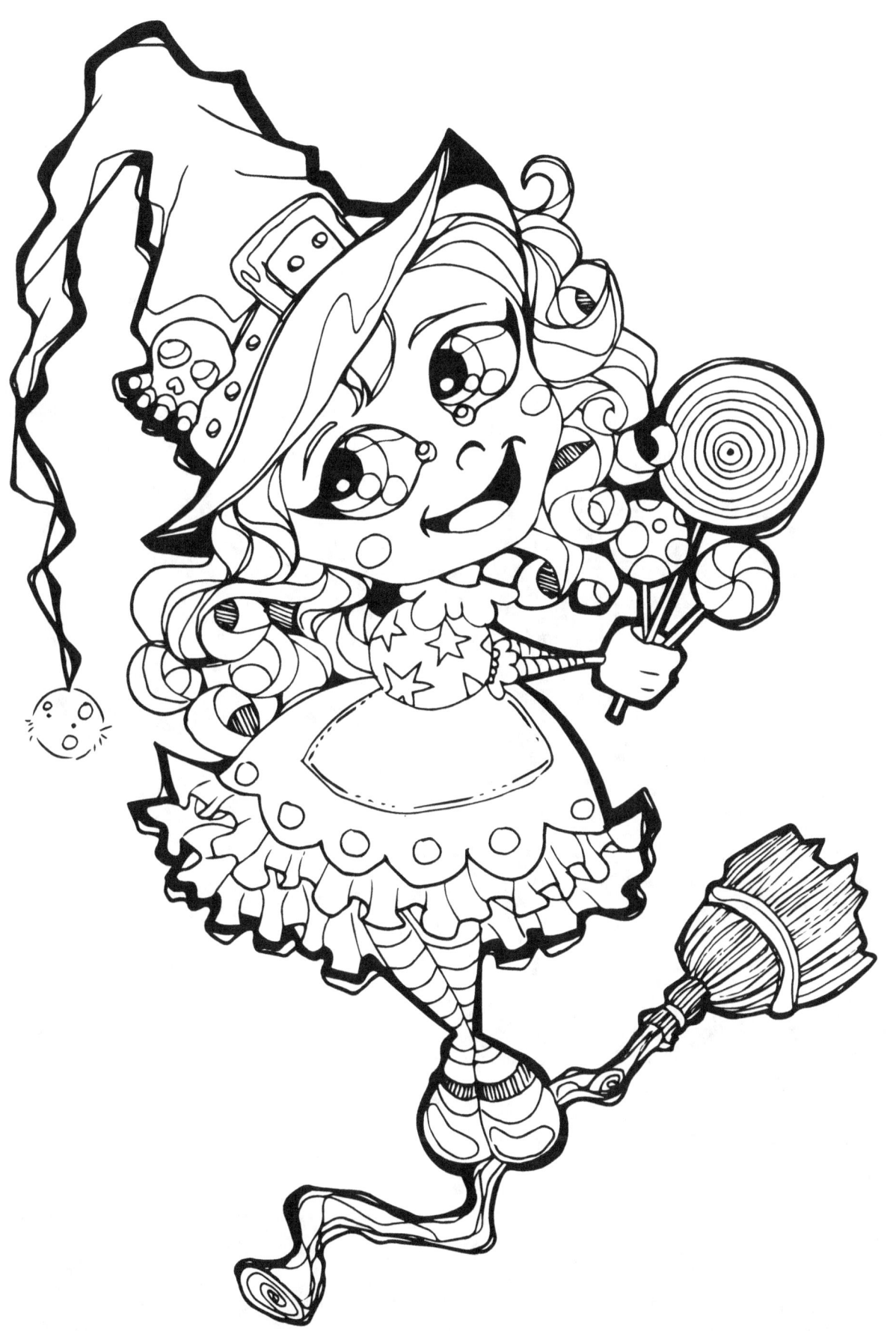

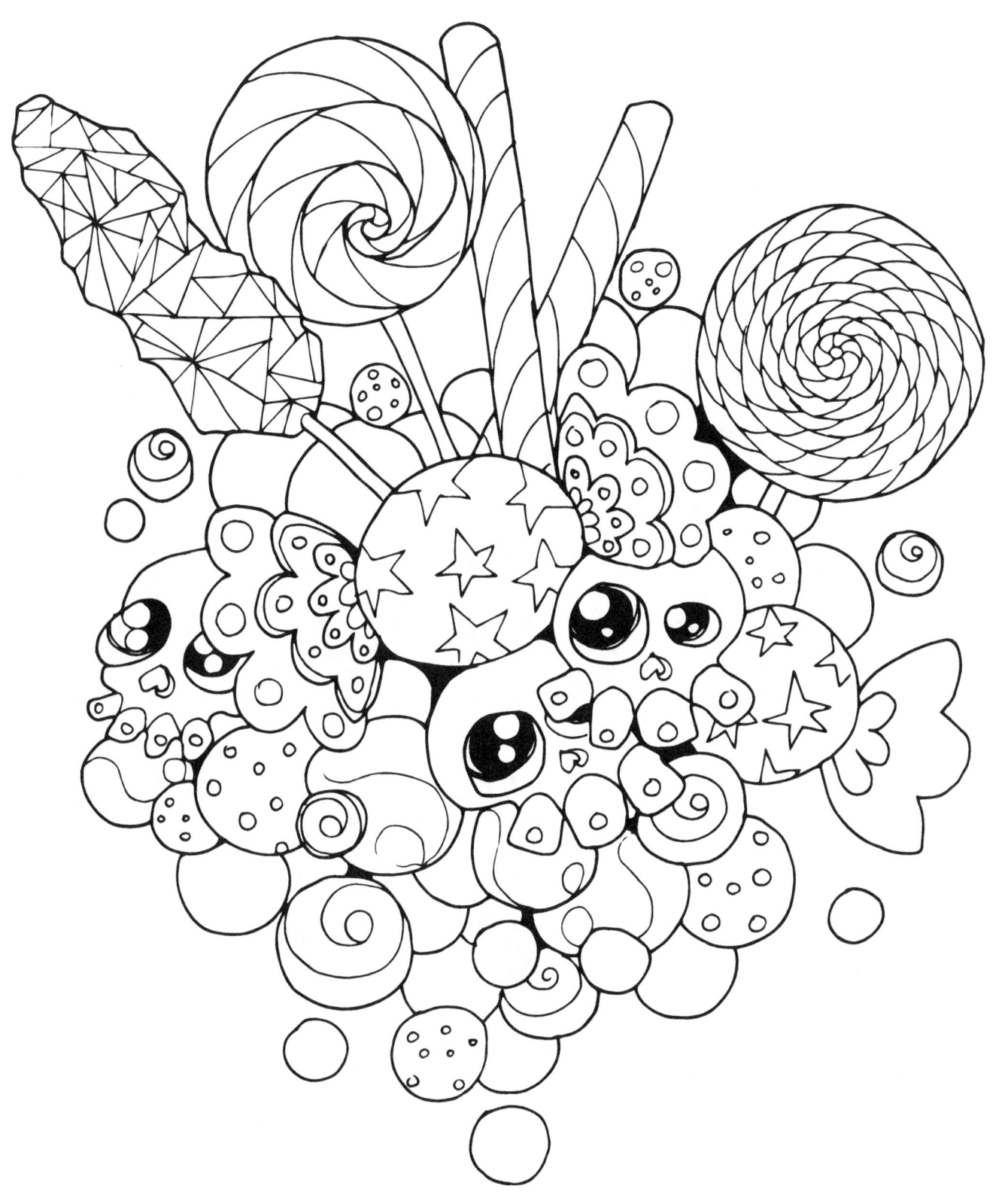

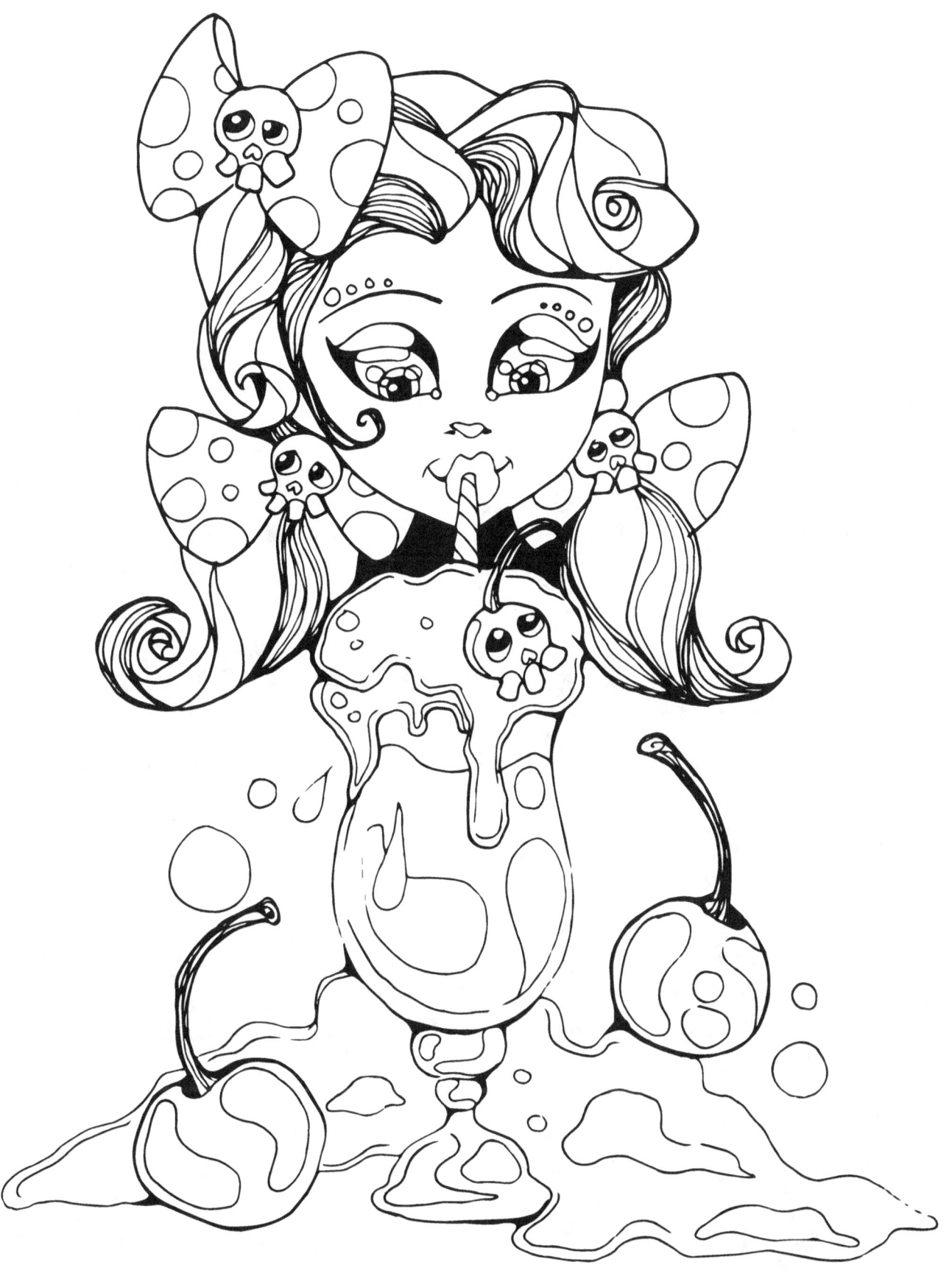

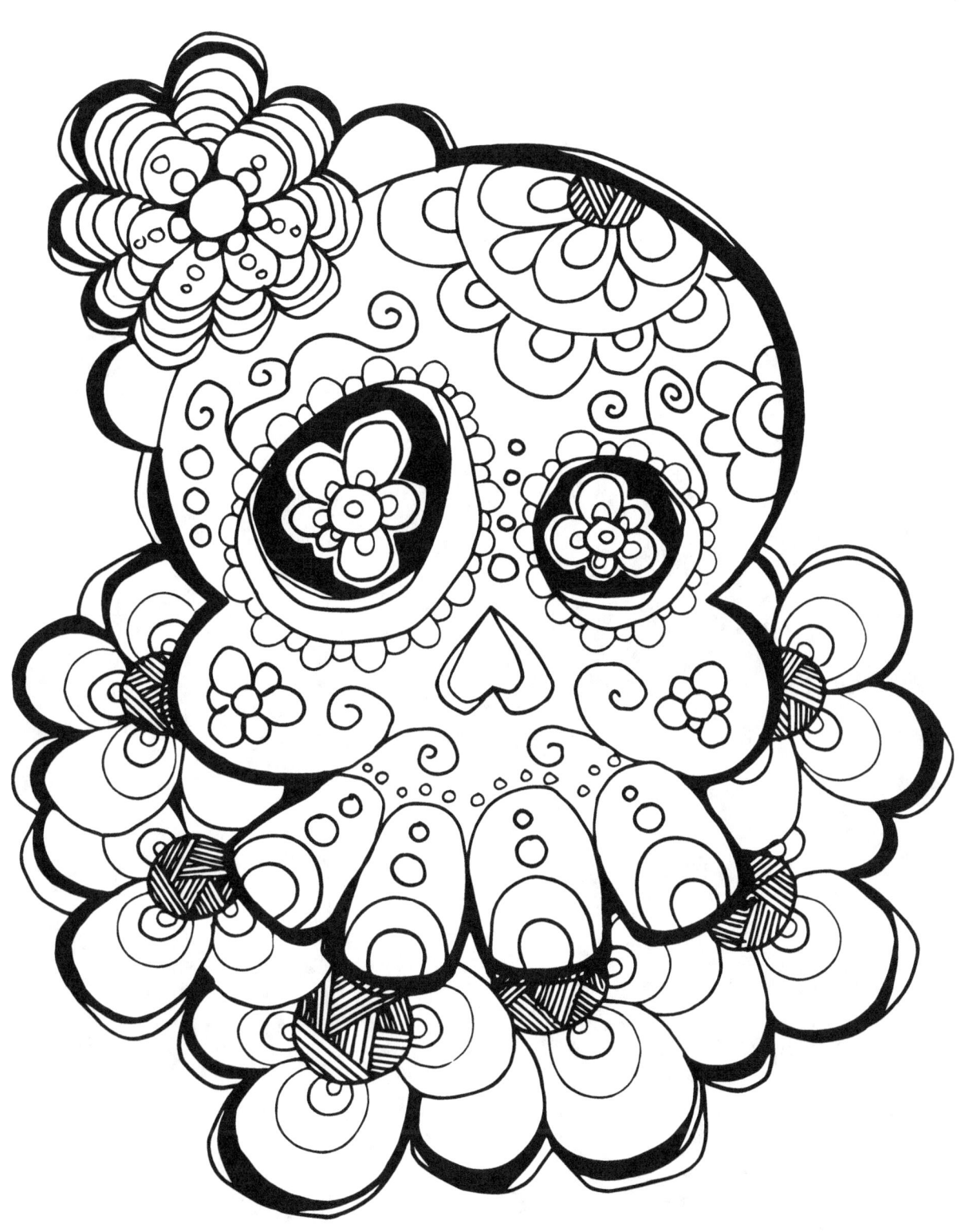

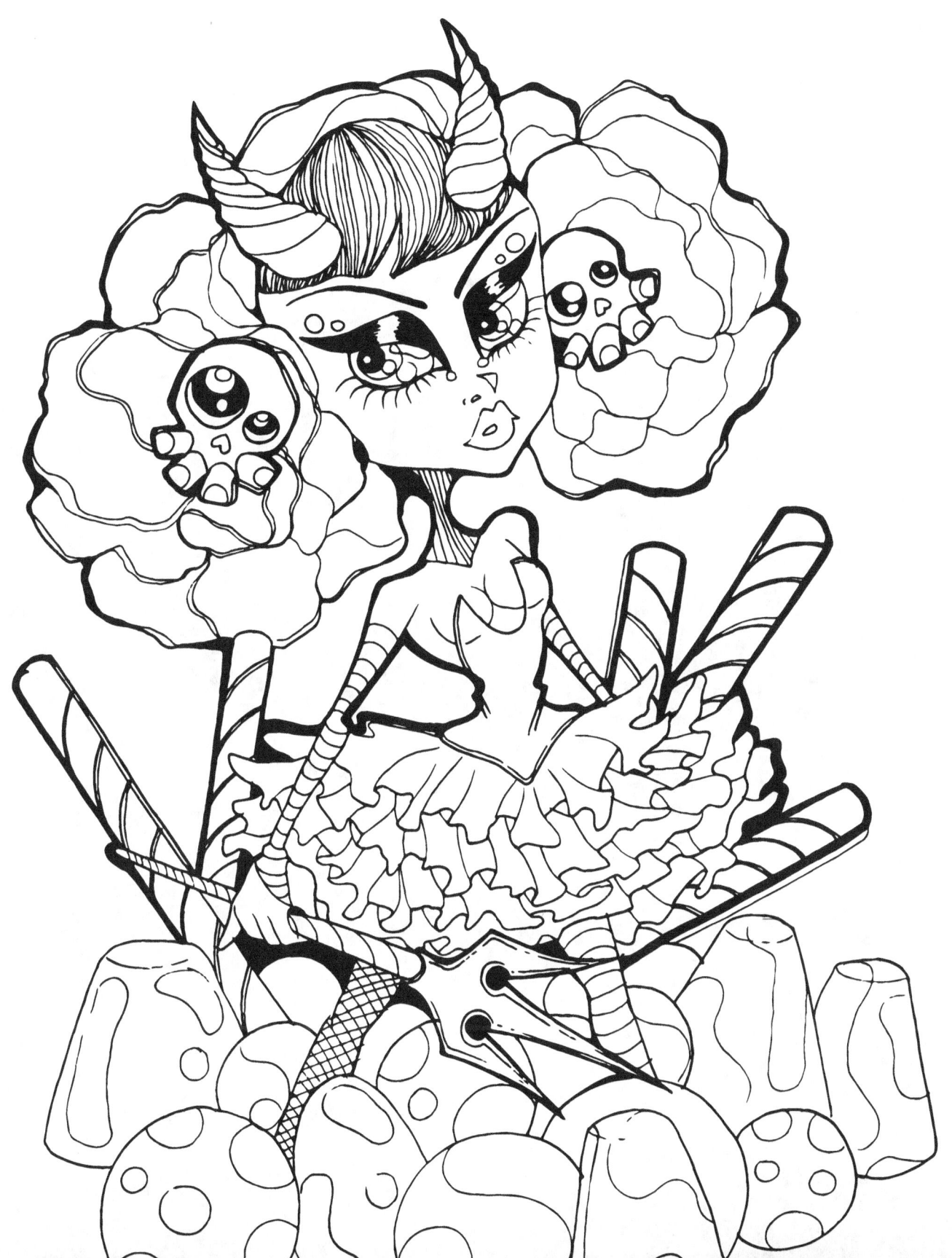

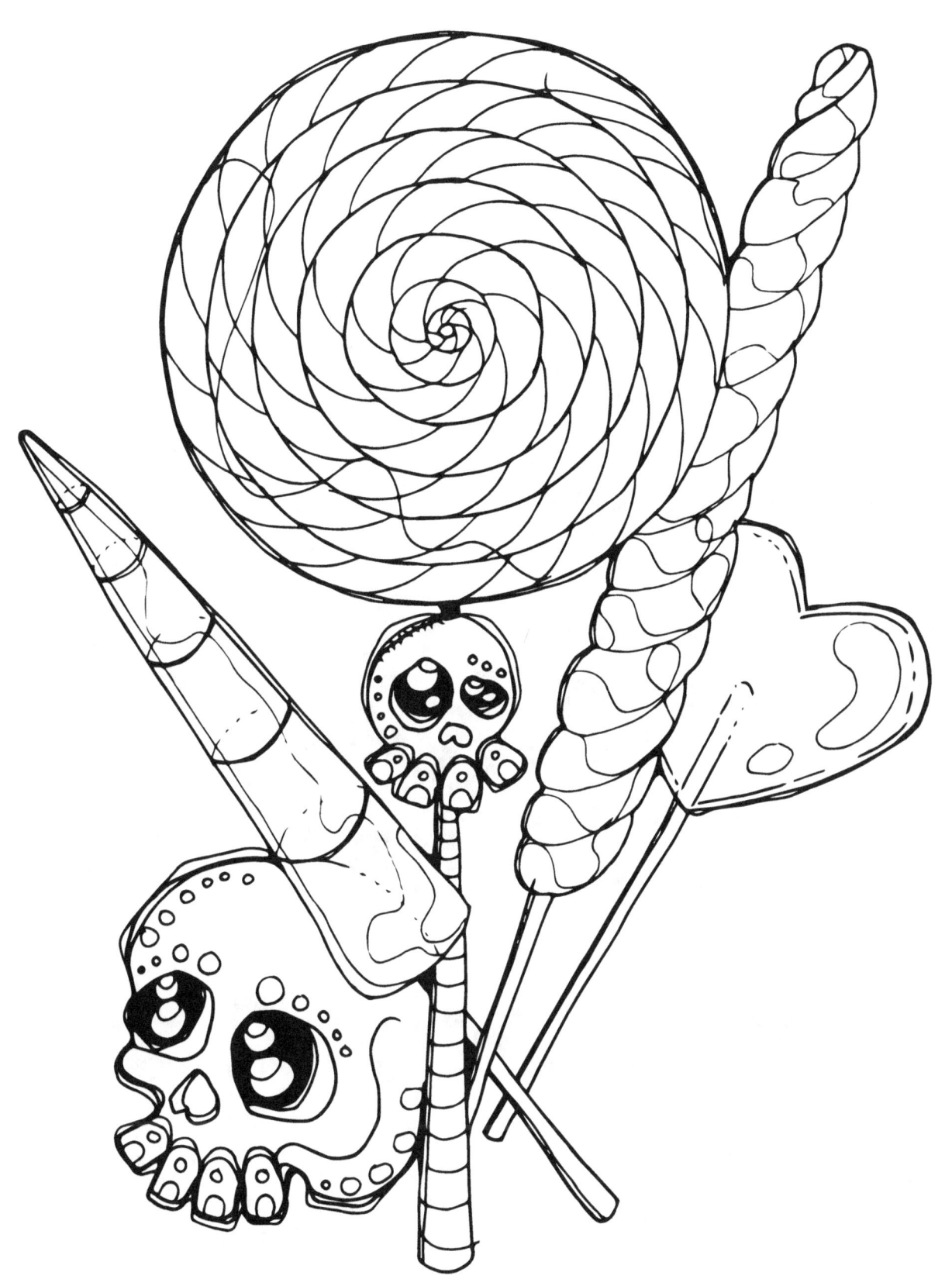

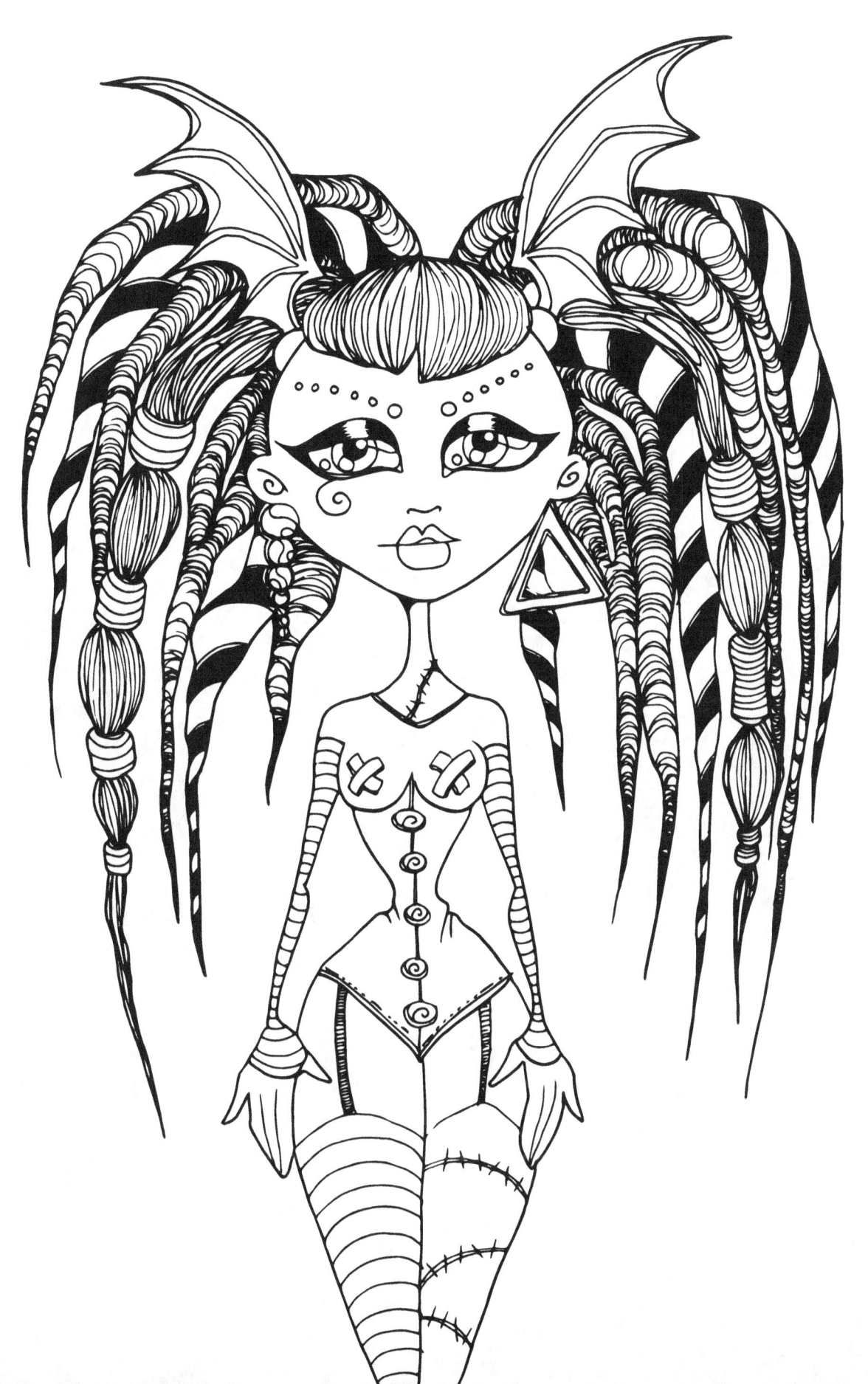

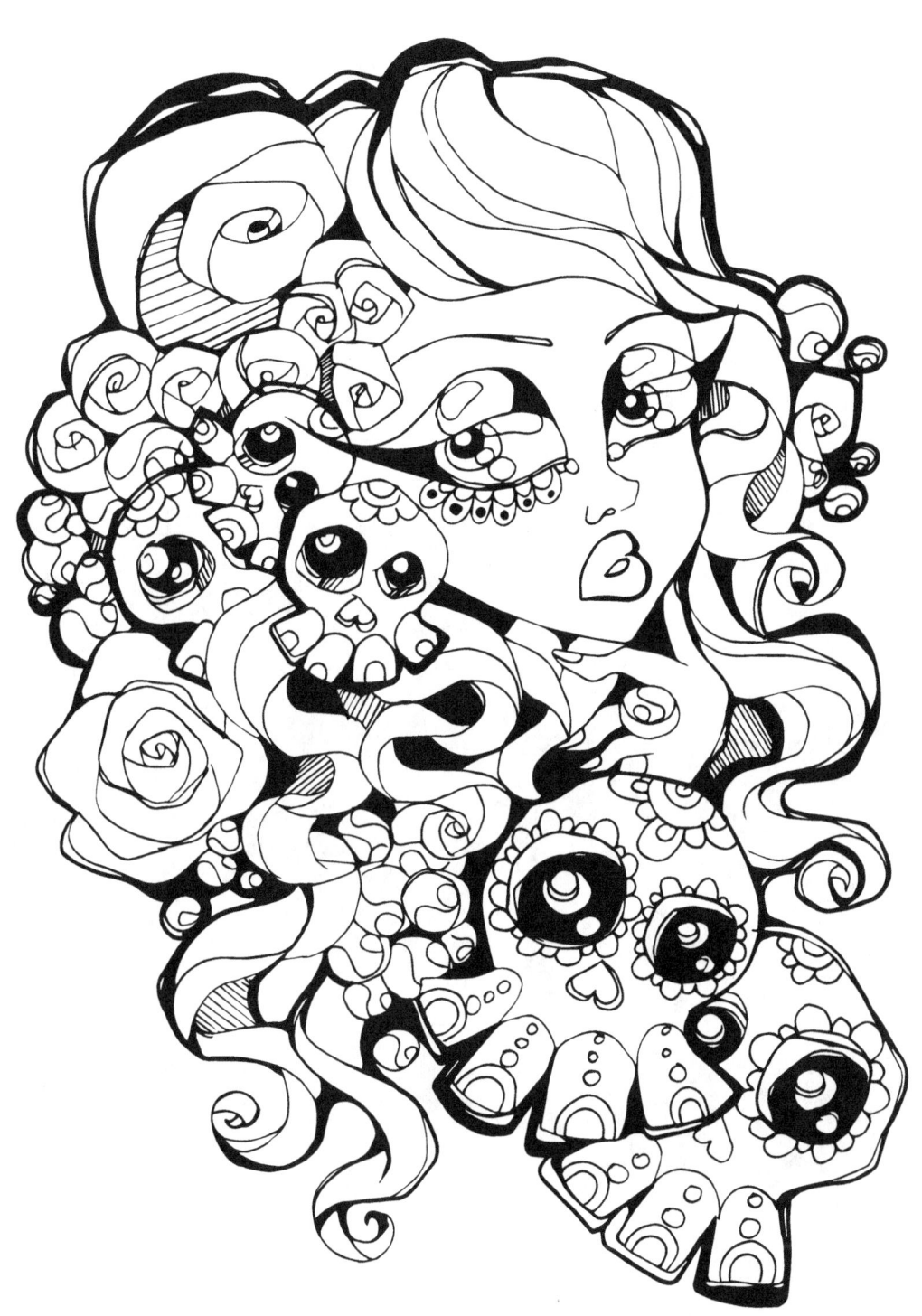

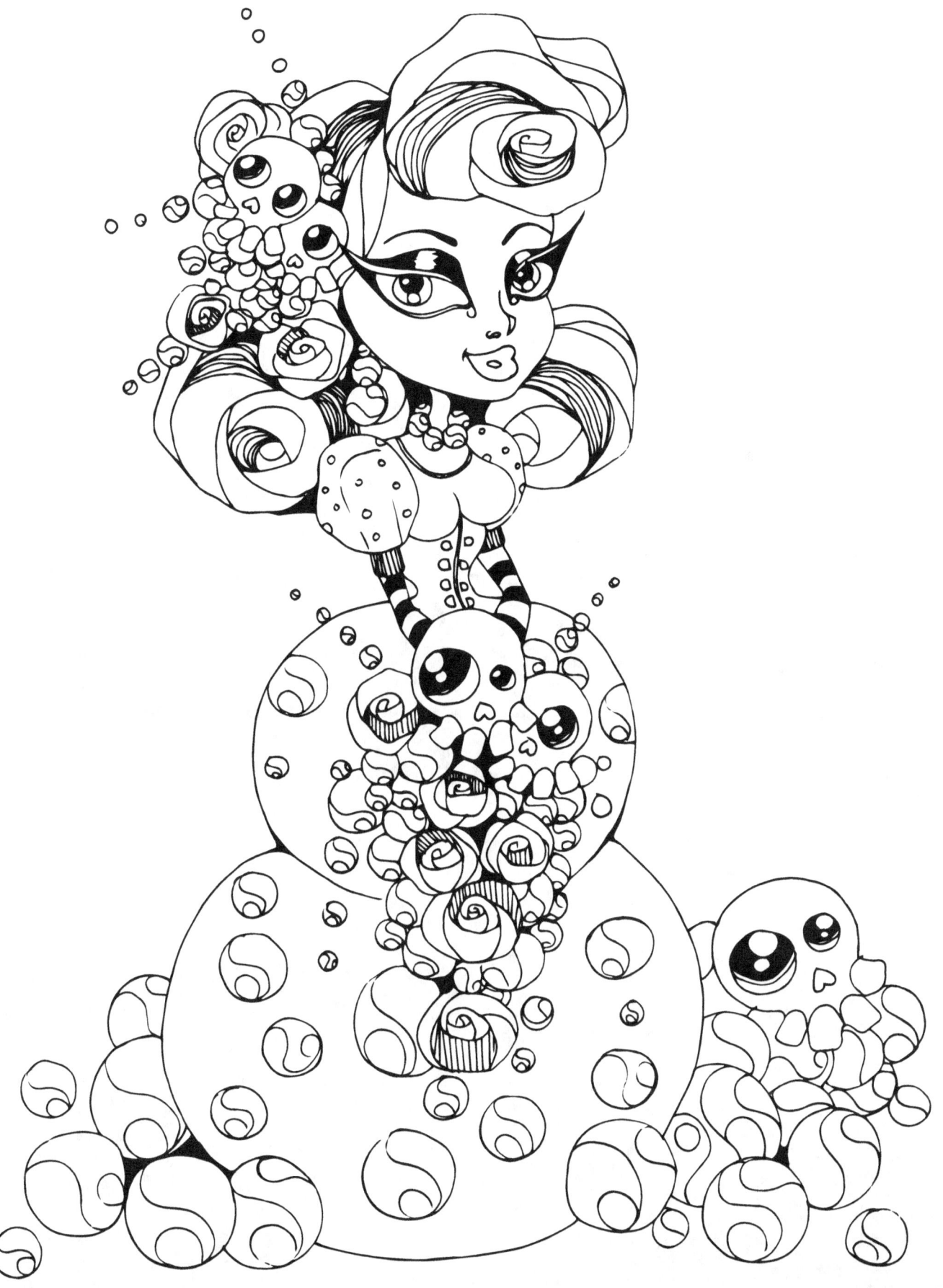

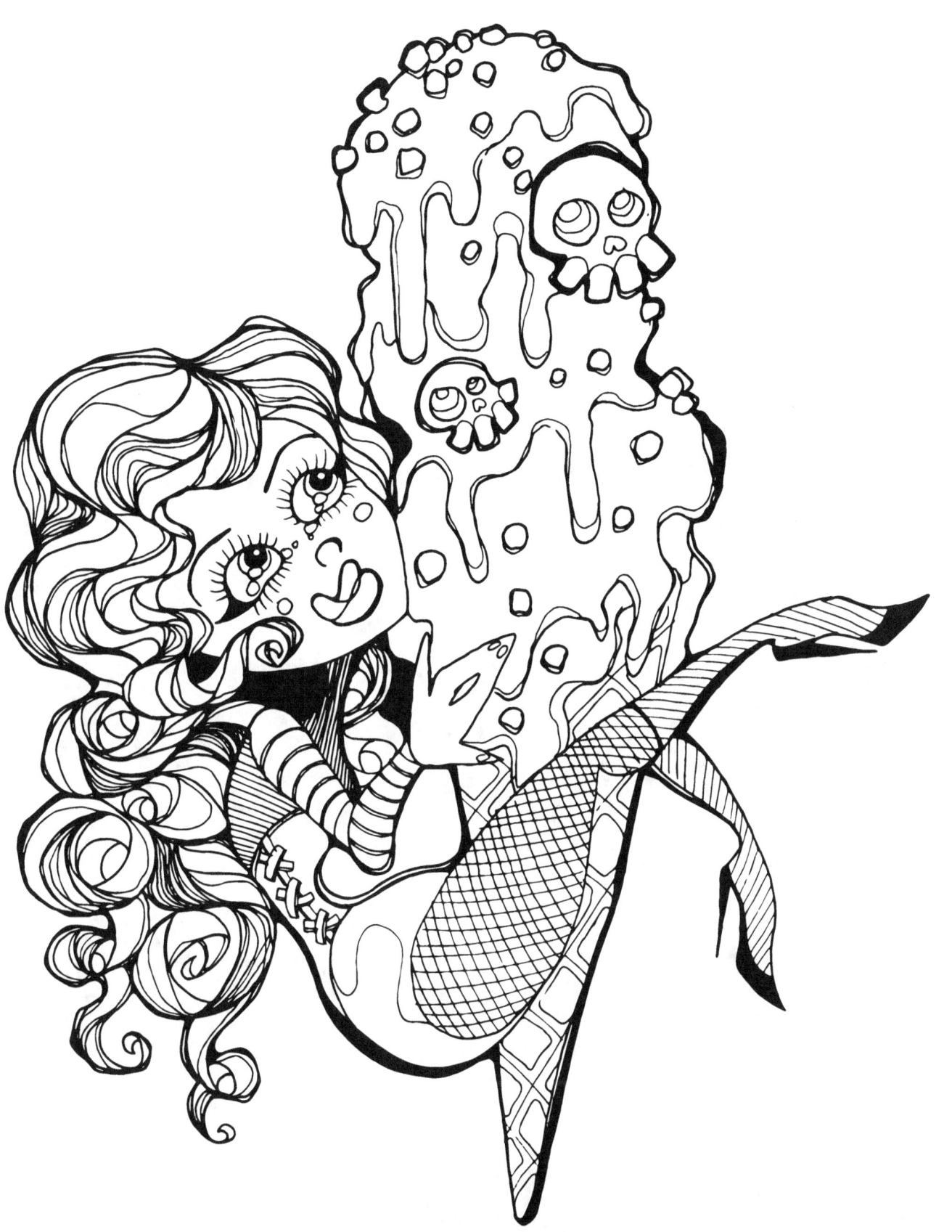

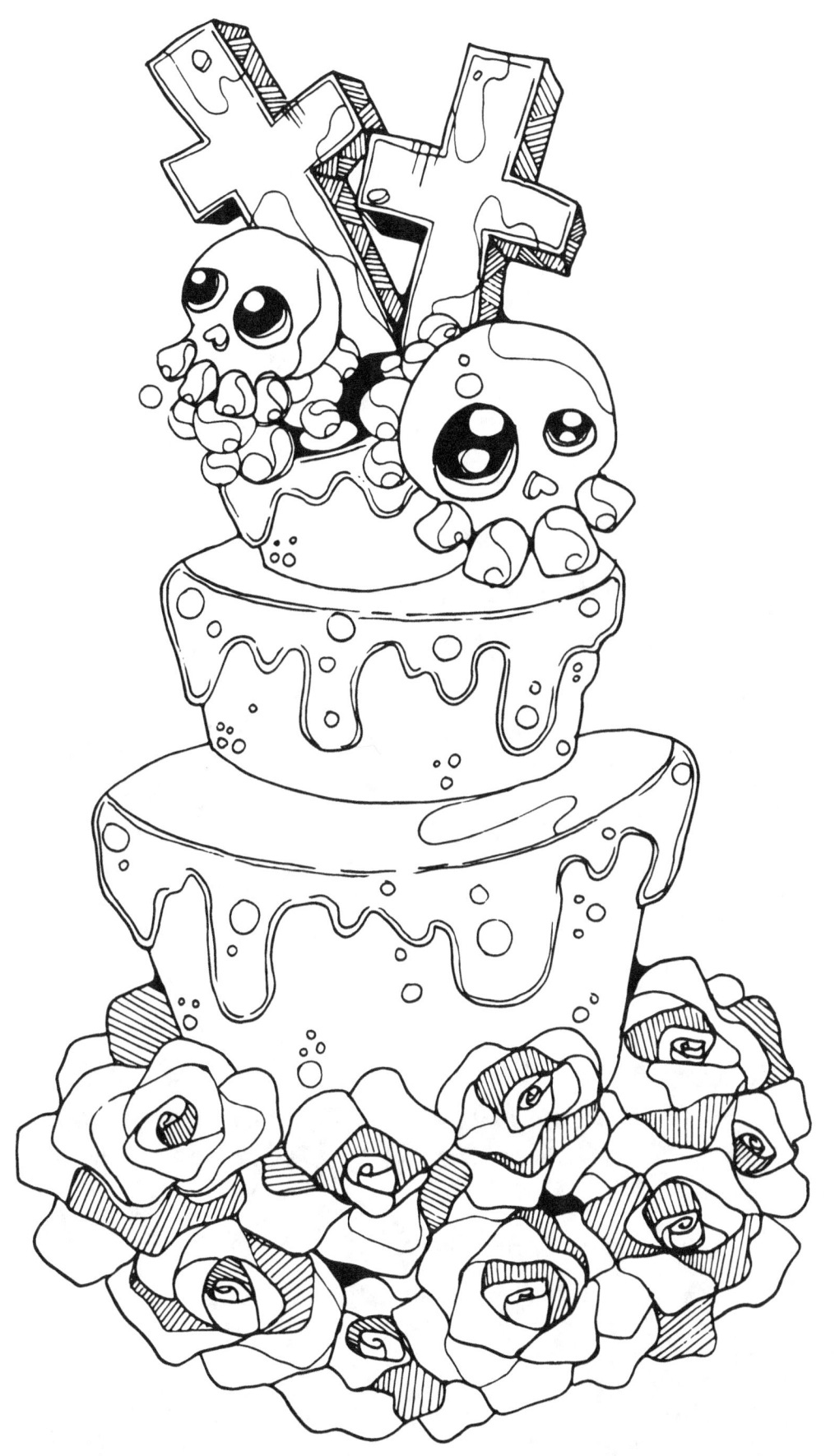

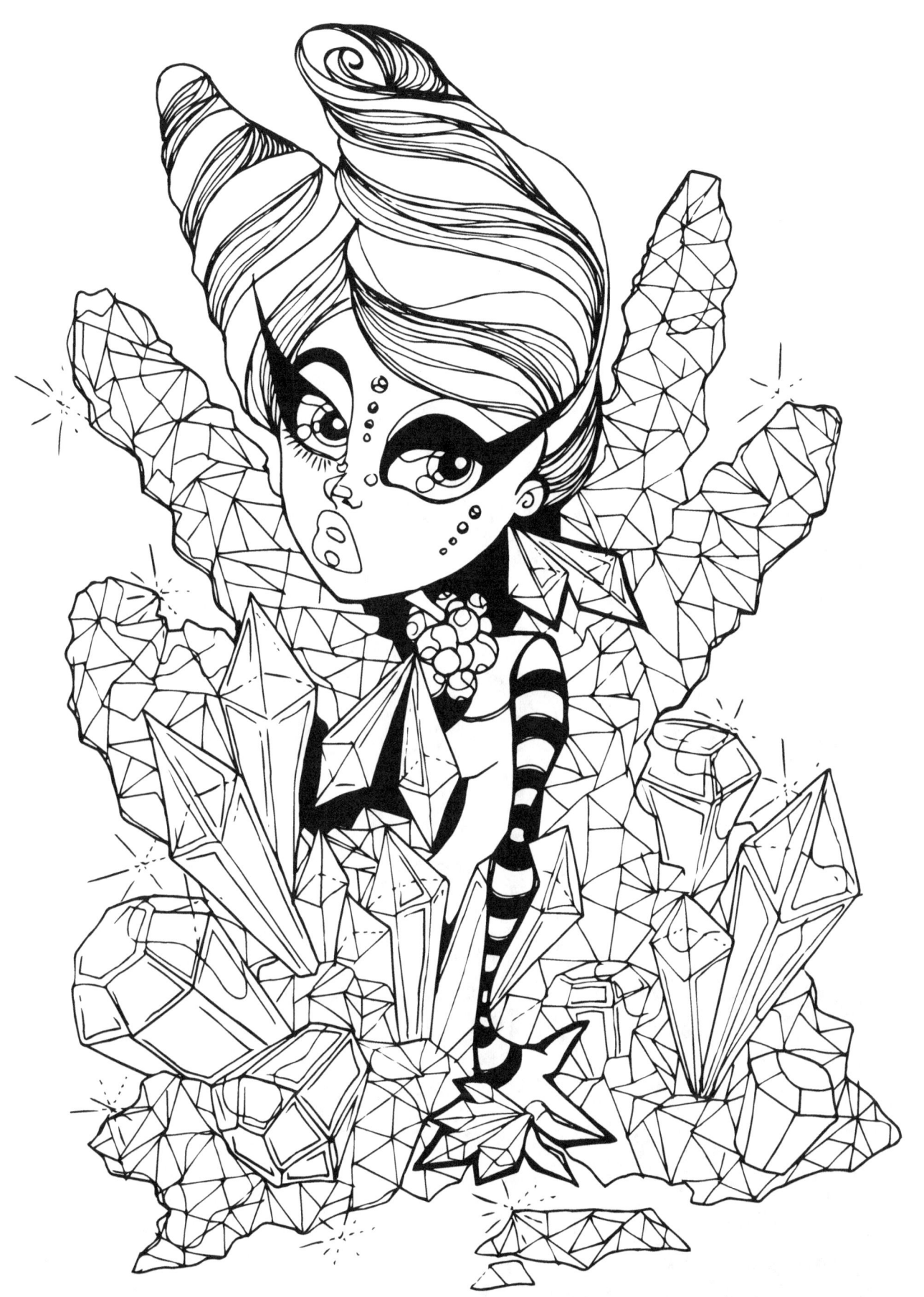

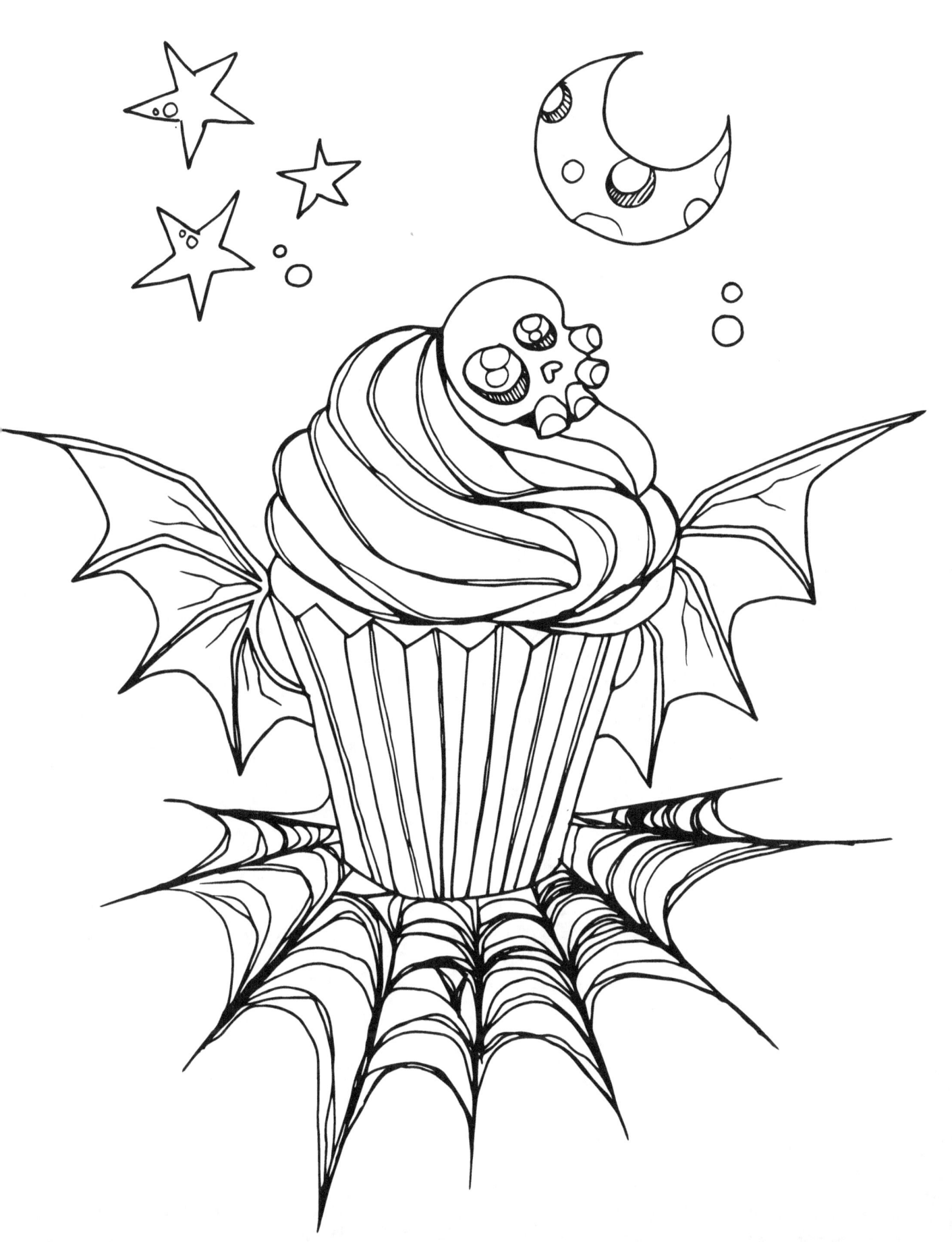

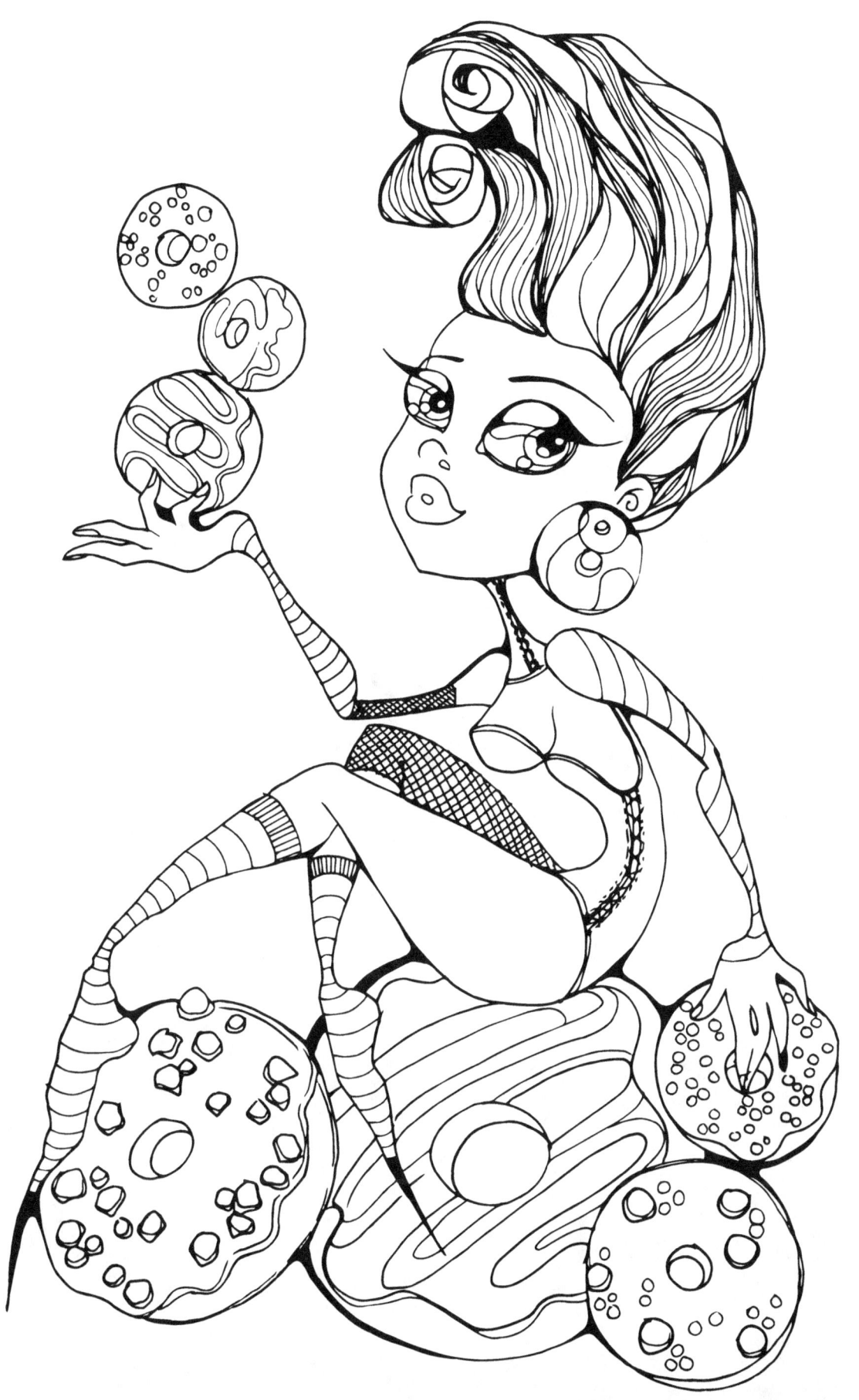

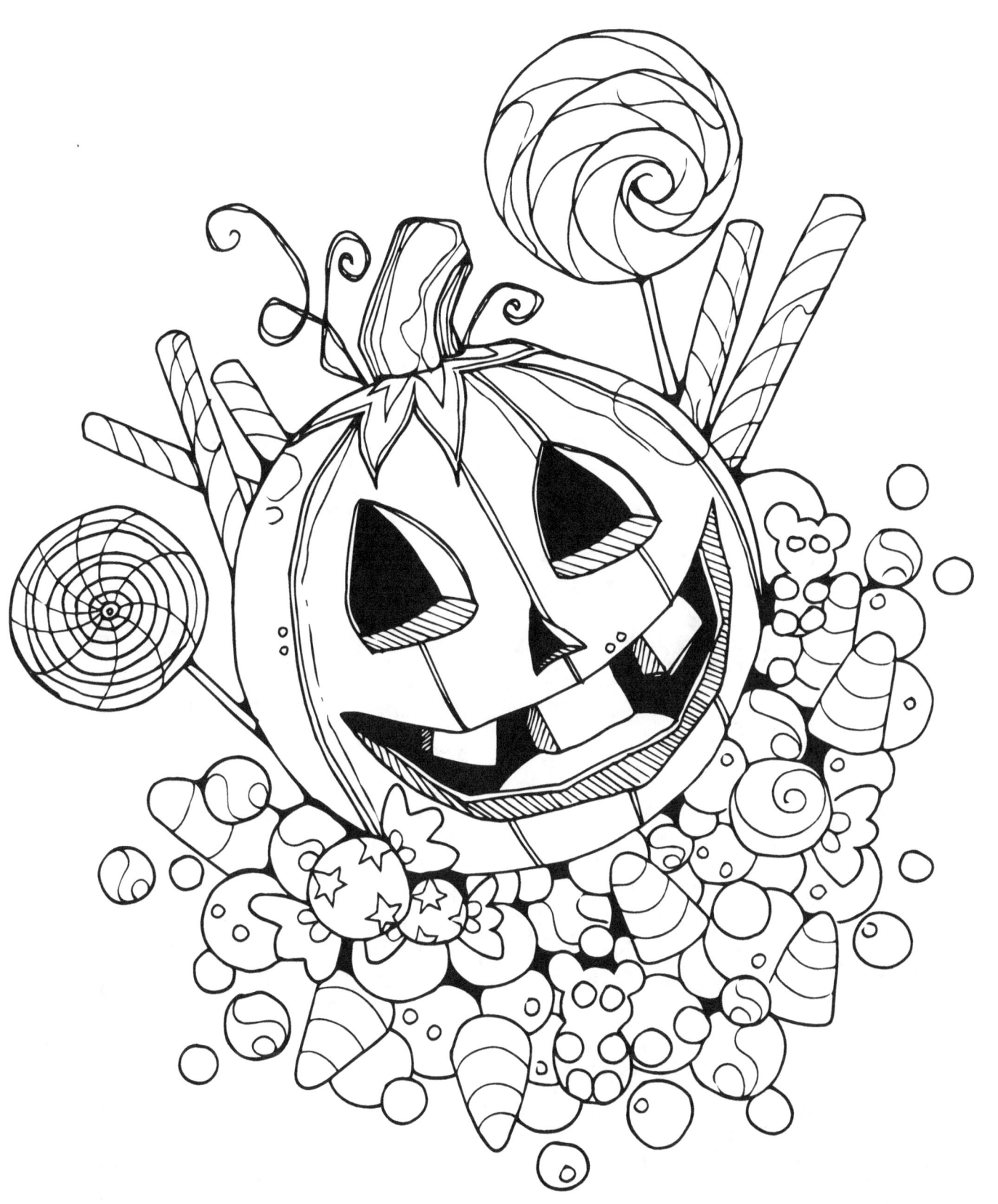

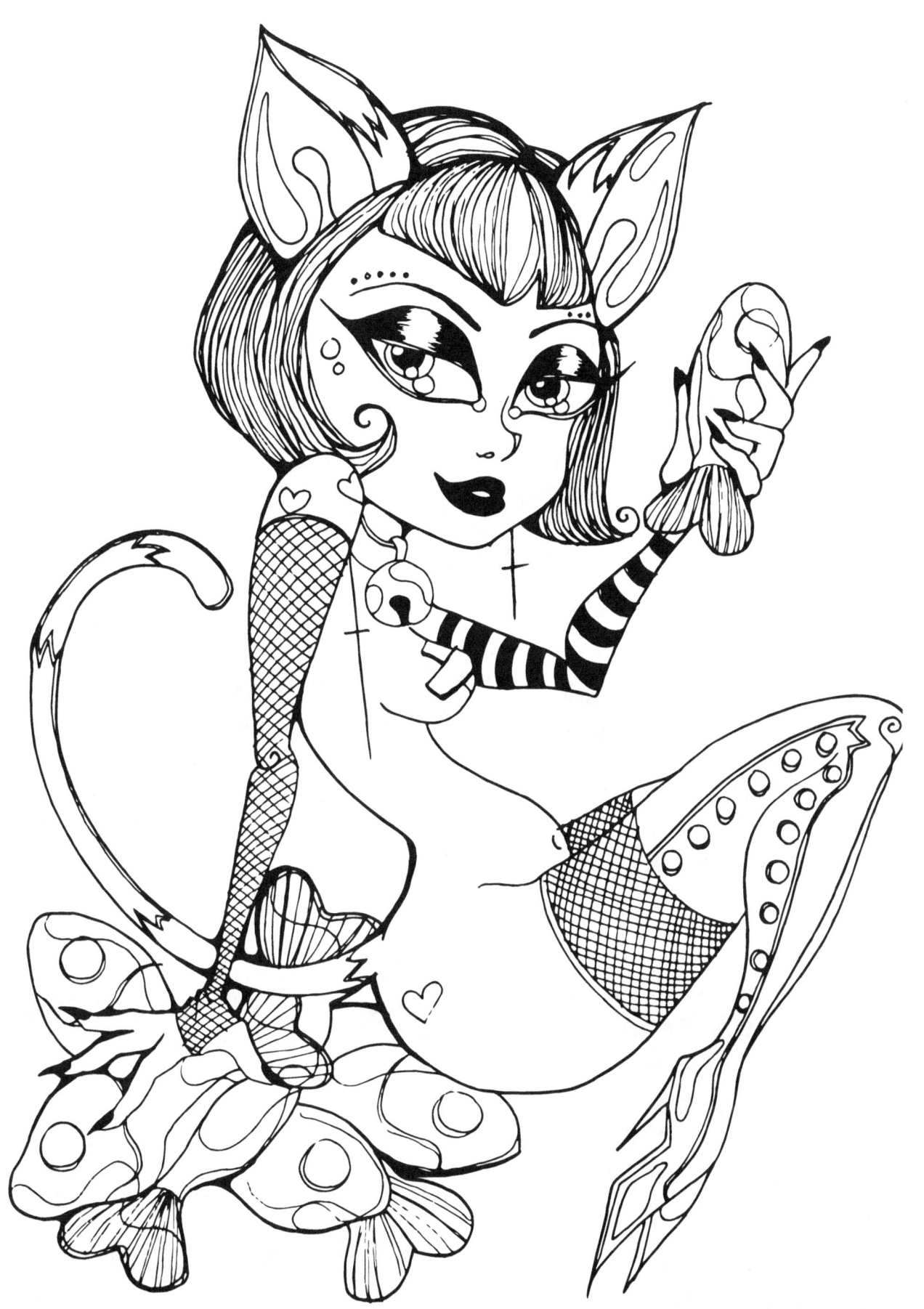

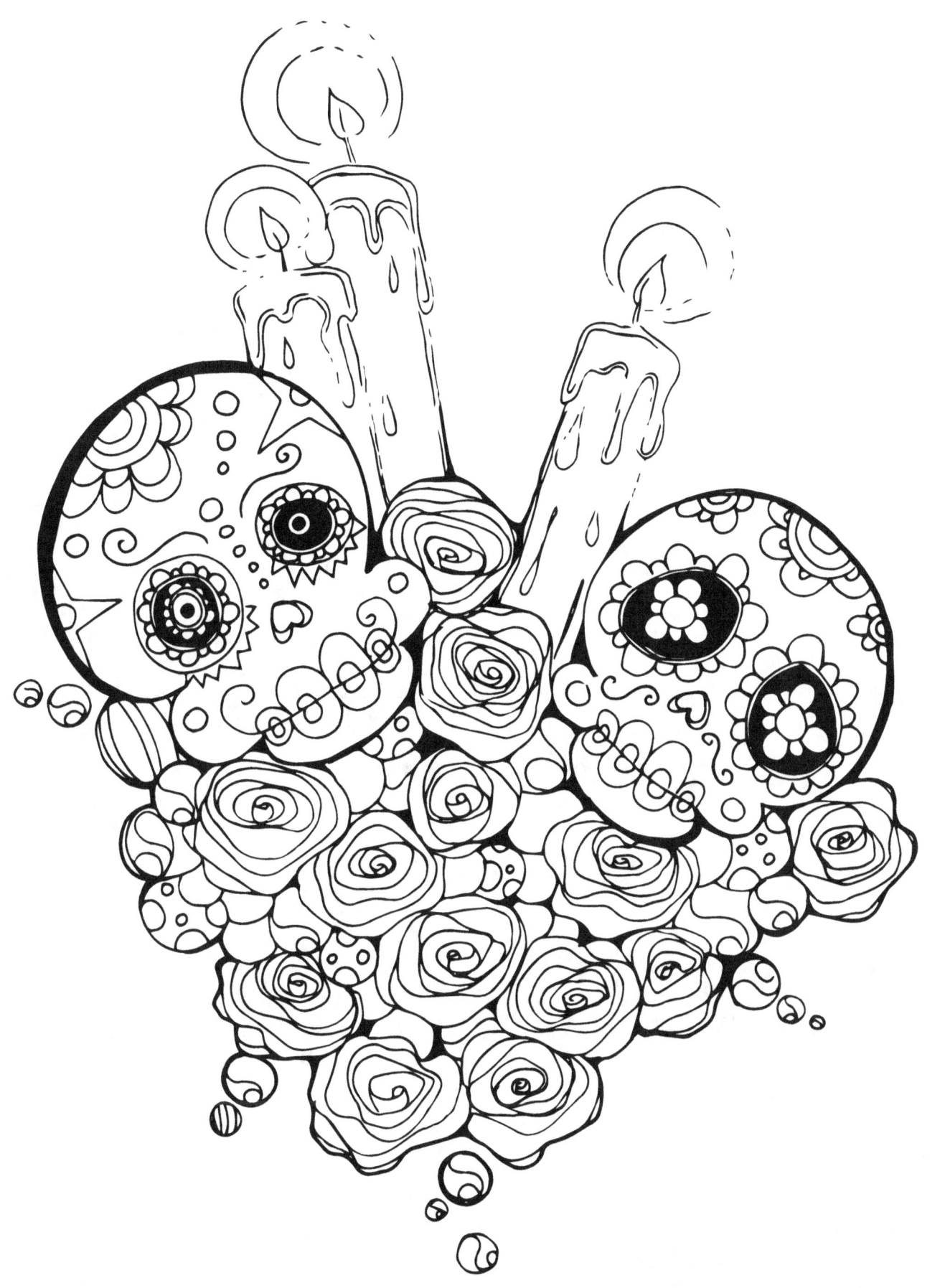

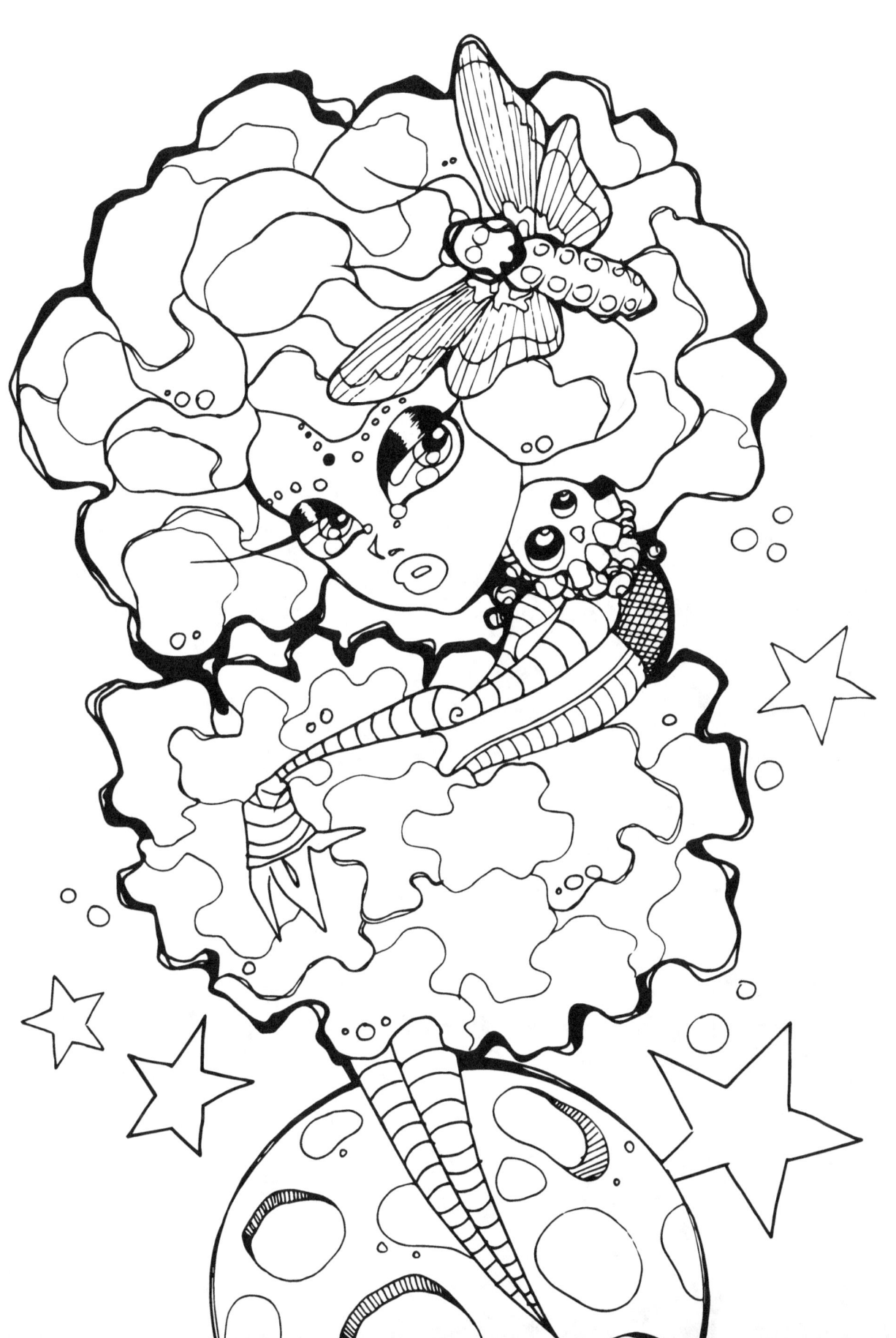

Test your art supplies on this page...

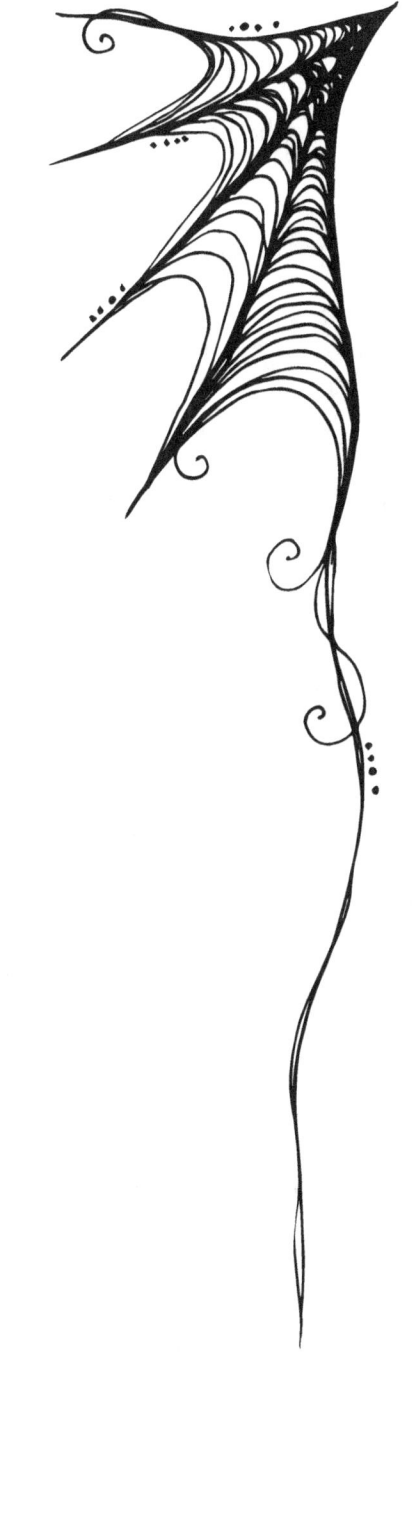

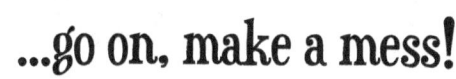
...go on, make a mess!

So, who is this chick?

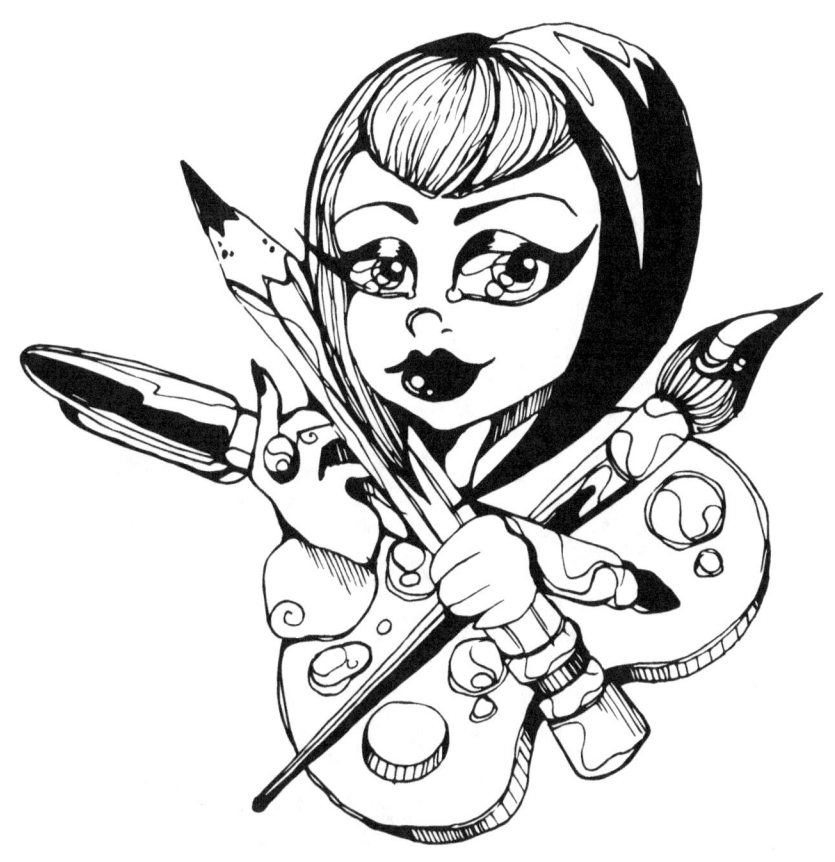

I'm Karla, a southern California based artist, designer and bookwormy tea addict. I spend my days designing, scribbling, daydreaming and hanging with my funky little mutt, Bentley. This is my first foray into coloring books and I am **SO** excited to share my work with you! I've had so much fun illustrating these pages and can't wait to see you work your magic on Spooky Sweets!

Join my art party online and share your pages (you know you wanna......)

Find me on:
• Facebook: ArtistKarlaMagana
• Instagram: karla_magana
(use #spookysweets to share your pages!)

karlamagana.com

www.ingramcontent.com/pod-product-compliance
Lightning Source LLC
Chambersburg PA
CBHW081301180526
45170CB00007B/2523